# The Ultimate Guide to British Pop Culture

# The Ultimate Guide to British Pop Culture

## Culture

### Live Like a Local

M Morgan

# Acknowledgements

Thanks to Ray, Kay and the girls for their contributions.

## Introduction

Being a tourist can be fun but it's even better when you can blend like a local.  Get the insight into local slangs, bargain shopping and sights.

# Phraseology

## 1P

One pence coin
*Pronounced* *'one pee'*
As in: I can't buy anything for *1P* even in the Pound Shop.

## 2P

Two pence coin (larger than 1p coin)
*Pronounced* *'two pee'*
As in: Its way more than *2P* per text.

## A fumble

Messing about (sexual)
*Pronounced* *'a fum·ble'*
As in: This bird and I had *a fumble* after the rave last night at her place.

## A knees up

To go for a drink mainly with a group
*Pronounced* *'a·neez·up'*

<u>As in</u>: Gonna go for *a knees up* with the blokes after work.

## Ainnit

Is that not so
*Pronounced* 'en·it'
<u>As in</u>: I gave you one already, *ainnit*, stop asking for more.

## Allotment

Plot of land used for small personal farm often located outside of the city areas
*Pronounced* 'a·lot·ment'
<u>As in</u>: My gran's *allotment* in Essex only has space for potatoes and corn.

## ASBO

<u>A</u>nti-<u>S</u>ocial <u>B</u>ehavior <u>O</u>rder- given by police to juniors for delinquent behavior
*Pronounced* 'az·bow'
<u>As in</u>: Jimmy got an *ASBO* for fighting at the party.

## Back in a tick

Will return soon
*Pronounced* *'bak in a tik'*
<u>As in</u>: Mom, I ran to the store but I will be
*back in a tick.*

## Bangers and mash

Sausage and mashed potato
*Pronounced* *'bang·az and mash'*
<u>As in</u>: Nothing beats some hot *bangers and*
*mash* with a pint.

## Bank holiday

Public holiday
*Pronounced* *'bank hol·ee·day'*
<u>As in</u>: Today is a *bank holiday* so the kids are
out of school.

## Barrister

Attorney (goes to court as an advocate)
*Pronounced* *'ba·ris·ta'*
<u>As in</u>: Mi *barrister* did a shoddy job
defending me, now I have court fees to pay.

## Battered

Beaten up (literal or figurative)
*Pronounced* *'bat·tad'*
<u>As in</u>: Man you look *battered*, work not going
well?

## Batty

Crazy
*Pronounced* *'bat·ee'*
<u>As in</u>: Having all these kids here with me
today is enough to make me *batty*.

## Bender

Pub crawl
*Pronounced* *'ben·dah'*
<u>As in</u>: The girls and I were on a nonstop
*bender* when on holiday.

## Benefits

Welfare
*Pronounced* *'ben·ee·fitz'*
<u>As in</u>: I got more *benefits* when I had the
second baby.

# Bike

Been around the block
*Pronounced* 'bike'
<u>As in</u>: Damn you're such a *bike*; every bloke
has had a piece.

# Bin

Garbage bin
*Pronounced* 'bin'
<u>As in</u>: Throw the garbage in the *bin* and
then take it out to the curb.

# Bird

Woman, girl, girlfriend
*Pronounced* 'bird'
<u>As in</u>: Me *bird* don't know that she isn't the
only one in my life.

# Blathered

Drunk
*Pronounced* 'bla·zthad'
<u>As in</u>: I was totally *blathered* last night; I
couldn't even find me flat.

## Blimey

Bloody hell
*Pronounced* *'bly·mee'*
As in: *Blimey*, her bum's so big the tires
went flat when she got in the car.

## Blinding

Really good, awesome
*Pronounced* *'blinding'*
As in: Getting the last tickets to the
hottest concert was *blinding*.

## Bloke

Boy, man
*Pronounced* *'bloke'*
As in: That *bloke* at the party had his hands
all over me.

## Bobby

Police
*Pronounced* *'bob·bee'*
As in: The *bobby* broke up the rave for
noise complaints.

# Bog

Toilet
*Pronounced* 'bog'
As in: The *bog* at the restaurant was a total mess.

# Bollocks

Shit (curse word)
*Pronounced* 'bol·locks'
As in: *Bollocks*, me car boot's busted.

# Bonkers

Mad, out of one's mind
*Pronounced* 'bunk·az'
As in: You drive me *bonkers* with your house music.

# Bonnet

Hood of a car
*Pronounced* 'bon·net'
As in: Don't sit on me car *bonnet*, you massive bum's gonna bust up me engine.

## Boot

Trunk of a car
*Pronounced* '*boot*'
<u>As in</u>: Put the buggy in the *boot*, I'll carry the baby in my arms.

## Boot sale

Jumble sale, yard sale
*Pronounced* '*boot sale*'
<u>As in</u>: I found the perfect pair of vintage jeans at a *boot sale* in Ipswich.

## Brilliant

Used when referring to something that's really good
*Pronounced* '*brill·ee·ant*'
<u>As in</u>: *Brilliant*, I just snagged an interview with the eccentric designer Alexander McQueen.

## Bubble and Squeak

A traditional English dish made with lightly fried vegetables left over from a roast dinner

*Pronounced* 'bub·ble and skweek'
<u>As in</u>: I made some *bubble and squeak* for tea before going to the pub with me mates.

## Bugger off

Go away
*Pronounced* 'bug·er·of'
<u>As in</u>: *Bugger off* you old slag, and leave me alone.

## Buggy

Baby stroller
*Pronounced* 'bug·ee'
<u>As in</u>: I'm selling the *buggy* at a boot sale when the baby starts walking.

## Bull bags

Testicles
*Pronounced* 'bull bagz'
<u>As in</u>: His shorts were so short and tight that you could see his mangy *bull bags*.

## Bullseye

50 pound note

*Pronounced* *'bullz·eye'*
<u>As in</u>: Those trousers weren't worth a
cockle much less a whole *bullseye*.

## Bum

Borrow
*Pronounced* *'bum'*
<u>As in</u>: Let me *bum* a fiver off you.

## Bum

Butt
*Pronounced* *'bum'*
<u>As in</u>: Your *bum* is not as bootilicious as
J.Lo's or Beyonce's.

## Bum off

Go away
*Pronounced* *'bum off'*
<u>As in</u>: Just *bum off*, I don't want to talk.

## Bunkup

To have sex
*Pronounced* *'bunk·up'*

As in: Best have a *bunkup* with an old pal than a stranger, ainnit?

## Buzz

Phone call
*Pronounced* 'buzz'
As in: Give me a *buzz* when you get back to the flat.

## Cab

Taxi
*Pronounced* 'kab'
As in: I need to grab a black *cab* to get to the city.

## Charlie

Cocaine
*Pronounced* 'char·lee'
As in: I almost got knicked for *Charlie* because of some chav slag.

## Chav

Common, ghetto
*Pronounced* 'chav'

As in: Wearing skaggy knickers is so *chav*.

# Cheeky

Rude
*Pronounced* 'cheek·ee'
As in: You *cheeky* monkey, you took my last cookie.

# Cheers

Thanks
*Pronounced* 'cheerz'
As in: *Cheers* mate, that's some capital bangers and mash.

# Chemist

Pharmacy
*Pronounced* 'kem· ist'
As in: Pop in the *chemist* and grab me some cough medicine.

# Chilly – billy

Scared, cowardly
*Pronounced* 'chill·ee – bill·ee'

As in: The *chilly-billy* copped out of riding the roller coasters at Euro-Disney.

## Chips

French fries
*Pronounced* 'chipz'
As in: Fish and *chips* are pretty much the iconic national dish of England.

## Chuck

Throw
*Pronounced* 'chuk'
As in: I didn't *chuck* out your ratty trainers even though I should have.

## Chuffed

Happy
*Pronounced* 'choft'
As in: I'm *chuffed* for you that you got the job.

## Cinema

Movies
*Pronounced* 'sin·ee·mah'

As in: Let's go to the *cinema* tomorrow, that new movie is out.

## Coat

Jacket
*Pronounced* 'koat'
As in: I'll need a new *coat* before winter is over.

## Cockle

10 pound note
*Pronounced* 'kok·uhl'
As in: It cost me a *cockle* for fish and chips in West End, blimey.

## Cockney

Slang spoken by some Londoners
*Pronounced* 'cock·nee'
As in: A *cockney* accent is often hard to understand for a non-Londoner.

## College

School you enter at approximately 16 after you finish GCSE exams

*Pronounced* 'kol·edge'

<u>As in</u>:  I hope to get into a good *college*, my mam would be so proud.

## Cosser

Police
*Pronounced* 'koss·a'
<u>As in</u>:  Damn *cosser*, bust up the rave just as it was getting hot.

## Cotton

Thread
*Pronounced* 'kot·ton'
<u>As in</u>:  The *cotton* from my jacket sleeve unraveled on the tube, how embarrassing.

## Council Tax

A civic tax assessed to everyone and is paid to cover public services such as trash removal etc...
*Pronounced* 'cown·sill tax'
<u>As in</u>:  Because I had to pay the *council tax* I'm only left with twenty quid.

## Crisps

Snacks like potato chips, corn chips etc
*Pronounced* 'krispz'
<u>As in</u>: Prawn *crisps* are so much better than barbeque or cheddar.

## CV

Curriculum vitae, resume
*Pronounced* 'cee·vee'
<u>As in</u>: I need to update my *CV* so I can apply for a job.

## Daft

Stupid, dumb
*Pronounced* 'daff·te'
<u>As in</u>: Don't be *daft*, of course the World Cup's in South Africa this year.

## Diary

Phone number log like PDA or actual diary for personal thoughts
*Pronounced* 'die·a·ree'
<u>As in</u>: I thought I put your number in my *diary* yesterday but I don't see it.

# Dimlo

Dumb, stupid, foolish
*Pronounced* *'dim·low'*
<u>As in</u>: He's a *dimlo*; you can't take what he says seriously.

# Dinky

Small and puny
*Pronounced* *'ding·kee'*
<u>As in</u>: That's such a *dinky* baby, I feel like she'll break if I hold her.

# Div

Stupid, foolish
*Pronounced* *'di·iv'*
<u>As in</u>: That's so *div*, I can't believe she did that.

# Dodgey

Uncertain, suspect
*Pronounced* *'dah·gee'*
<u>As in</u>: I had me some *dodgey* burgers for tea and spent the night in the bog.

## Dog's bollocks

Something really good
*Pronounced* '*dogs bol·lox*'
<u>As in</u>: Winning tickets to the World Cup was the *dog's bollocks*.

## Dole

Welfare, government assistance
*Pronounced* '*doe·luh*'
<u>As in</u>: For some getting on the *dole* is a higher priority than landing a job. Leave the *dole* for those who really need help lazy asses.

## Dolled up

Dressed and ready for a party or going out
*Pronounced* '*dolled up*'
<u>As in</u>: I got all *dolled up* for the party and he stood me up.

## Dosh

Money
*Pronounced* '*doshe*'
<u>As in</u>: The dole hardly gives enough *dosh* to cover the bills and grab a pint.

## Dosser

Lazy person, unwelcome visitor, unmotivated individual
*Pronounced* 'doss·a'
As in: It's the *dossers* that are draining the dole instead of getting off their asses to find jobs.

## Dossing

Sitting around doing nothing
*Pronounced* 'dos·sin'
As in: *Dossing* is the favorite past time of most benefits recipients like Britain many uber young parents and grandparents.

## Down the boozer

At the pub
*Pronounced* 'down the booz·a'
As in: Are you going *down the boozer* after work today?

## Estate agent

Realtor
*Pronounced* 'estaate ay·gent'

As in: I popped into the *estate agent's* office to look for a new flat.

## Fag

Cigarette
*Pronounced* 'fahg'
As in: Can I bum a *fag* off you; I haven't had a smoke in a while?

## Fancy

To like someone or something; to take notice of something
*Pronounced* 'fan·cee'
As in: *Fancy* that, you're letting me take the last peppermint patty?
As in: Which of those blokes do you *fancy*, I think the one on the end is blinding.

## Fanny

Vagina
*Pronounced* 'fan·ee'
As in: Me *fanny* want nothing to do with you willy.

# Flat

Apartment
*Pronounced* 'flaht'
<u>As in</u>: My *flat* in Colchester was dirt cheap.
Four bullseyes a pop aint bad ainnit.

# For hire

For rent (ie: car)
*Pronounced* 'for high·er'
<u>As in</u>: Please find a car *for hire* so I can get
to the airport.

# Get his/her end away

To have sex
*Pronounced* 'get his/her end away'
<u>As in</u>: Olivia wants to *get her end away*
tonight; it's been too long since she had
some.

# Get off

Go away
*Pronounced* 'get off'
<u>As in</u>: I wish that slag would just *get off*, no
one needs such nastiness.

## Going on a piss

To go out with the intention of getting drunk
*Pronounced* *'going on a piss'*
<u>As in</u>:  I'm getting all dolled up and going on a piss with the gals later.

## Goss

Gossip
*Pronounced* *'gos'*
<u>As in</u>:  The office *goss* about me being a dosser is a total lie.

## Grass

Snitch, informant, tattletale
*Pronounced* *'gr·ass'*
<u>As in</u>:  I would never be a *grass*, ratting on my mates is not an option.

## Gutted

Sad
*Pronounced* *'gut·hed'*
<u>As in</u>:  Man, I'm *gutted* you lost the race.

# Half License

Convenience store specializing in alcohol
sales
*Pronounced* *'awf lie·cense'*
<u>As in</u>: I'll stop by the *half license* to pick up
some beer for the party.

# Hen night/Hen do

Bachelorette party
*Pronounced* *'hen night' or 'hen do'*
<u>As in</u>: My *hen night* was a week before the
wedding and the girls got a stripper for me.

# High street

Main road (depending on where you're
located it leads directly to London)
*Pronounced* *'high street'*
<u>As in</u>: The *high street* from Thornton Heath
to Brixton is forever congested.

# Holiday

Vacation
*Pronounced* *'hol·ee·day'*
<u>As in</u>: If I don't get to go on *holiday* to
Ibiza this summer I'll go absolutely batty.

# Hoover

Vacuum
*Pronounced* 'hoo·vah'
<u>As in</u>: I always *hoover* the house before guests arrive.

# Ice lollies

Icy pops, frozen flavored ice snacks
*Pronounced* 'ice loll·eez'
<u>As in</u>: I love grape flavored *ice lollies* when it's hot outside.

# Jacks

5 pound note
*Pronounced* 'jax'
<u>As in</u>: Spot me *jacks* so I can grab something to eat.

# Jock

Scottish person (may or may not be insulting)
*Pronounced* 'jok'
<u>As in</u>: I had a brawl with a *jock* at the pub over a pint last night.

# Jumper

Sweater top
*Pronounced* 'jum·pa'
<u>As in:</u> I found the cutest pink *jumper* at H&M yesterday.

# Junk

Bank
*Pronounced* 'junk'
<u>As in</u>: I'm going to the *junk* to get some extra cash.

# Keen

To really like something/someone
*Pronounced* 'keen'
<u>As in:</u> I'm *keen* on that dress, it's really lovely.

# Kippers & Beans

Common English breakfast (fish with baked beans) can include fried eggs, toast and fried plantains (my twist) on the side
*Pronounced* 'kip·herz & beenz'

<u>As in</u>: My mom always makes *kippers and beans* for breakfast on Sundays when she's home.

## Kitchen paper

Paper towel
*Pronounced* 'kitchen pay·pa'
<u>As in</u>: Grab some *kitchen paper* and clean up this mess you made.

## Kitchen roll

Paper towel
*Pronounced* 'kitch·hen roll'
<u>As in</u>: I didn't know that Bounty *kitchen roll* wasn't popular in London.

## Knackered

Tired
*Pronounced* 'nak·ad'
<u>As in</u>: After the club last night I was totally *knackered.*

## Knick

Police station
*Pronounced* 'nik'
As in: I called the *knick* to report the
robbery but the bobby acted like I stole

## Knick

Steal
*Pronounced* 'nik'
As in: Getting your dosh *knicked* at a rave
can be quite a drag.

## Knicked

Arrested
*Pronounced* 'nikt'
As in: I got *knicked* last night for driving
drunk.

## Knickers

Panties
*Pronounced* 'nick·az'
As in: My new black sexy *knickers* from Ann
Summers are all lace.

# Knob

Penis
*Pronounced* *'nob'*
As in: Keep your *knob* in your pants, even the slappers don't want it.

# Knockers

Boobs
*Pronounced* *'nok·hers'*
As in: Her *knockers* kept popping out of her top as she did the drunken wobble.

# Lay-about

Lazy person, unmotivated individual
*Pronounced* *'lay about'*
As in: Stop being such a *lay about*, get off your ass and get a job.

# Legless

Stupid drunk
*Pronounced* *'leg·less'*
As in: You drank yourself *legless* with the girls last night at the pub and barely stumbled home.

## Leisure center

Community center
*Pronounced* 'leh·shur cen·ter'
As in: The Stratham *leisure center* offers swimming lessons for babies.

## Lift

Elevator
*Pronounced* 'lift'
As in: Take the *lift* up to me flat, it's on the third floor.

## Locked up

Closed, arrest
*Pronounced* 'lokt up'
As in: Jett got *locked up* last night for fighting at the rave.

## Longon

100 pound note
*Pronounced* 'long·on'
As in: *Longons* are not common British currency.

## Loo

Toilet
_Pronounced_ _'lou'_
<u>As in</u>:  The _loos_ by the underground are
pretty manky at times, I wouldn't use them.

## Manky

Ugly, gross, unsuitable
_Pronounced_ _'mang·kee'_
<u>As in</u>:   I found a _manky_ little cat on the car
boot this morning.

## Mate

Friend
_Pronounced_ _'mayt'_
<u>As in</u>:  Hey me and me _mates_ are gonna meet
up later.

## Mi

My
_Pronounced_ _'m·i'_
<u>As in</u>: _Mi_ readies are gone as soon as I get
paid.

# Minga

Ugly
_Pronounced_ 'min·gah'
<u>As in</u>: Lila's _minga_ mutt' so pathetic. I'm surprised she adopted it.

# Minge

Vagina
_Pronounced_ 'min·gee'
<u>As in</u>: I always make sure to shave my _minge_ before a hot date. You never know where it will end up.

# Mingy

Doesn't look good, ugly
_Pronounced_ 'min·gee'
<u>As in</u>: That cat looks so _mingy_, it's amazing it got adopted.

# Moan

Complain
_Pronounced_ 'moe·own'
<u>As in</u>: Stop _moaning_, dinner will be ready in a minute.

## Mock up

Mess up
*Pronounced* 'mok up'
<u>As in</u>: Please don't *mock up* mi room, I just cleaned it.

## Mobile

Cell phone
*Pronounced* 'moe·bile
<u>As in</u>: I can make unlimited calls on my pay-as-you-go *mobile*.

## MP

Ministers of parliament
*Pronounced* 'em pee'
<u>As in</u>: The new *MPs* in Parliament are elected by the people but serve their own interests.

## Mug

Idiot, fool
*Pronounced* 'mmugg'
<u>As in</u>: You freaking *mug*, you bought a fake Rolex for £100 and thought it was real!

## Mug or Mugging me off

Making fun of me, mocking me
*Pronounced* *'mmugg'* or *'mmugging me off'*
As in: Stop *mugging me off*, I am serious
that Teen Wolf is a classic movie.

## Muggly

Ugly
*Pronounced* *'mm·ugly'*
As in: Don't wear that *muggly* jumper, it
makes you look like my nan.

## Mum

Mother
*Pronounced* *'mum'*
As in: Me *mum* and I went to the boot sale
and bought a gorgeous baby buggy.

## Nan

Grandmother
*Pronounced* *'nan'*
As in: *Nan* and I went to a boot sale to buy
some old records.

## News agent

Convenience store – limited alcohol sale
*Pronounced* *'news ay·gent'*
<u>As in</u>: I picked up a copy of Cosmo at the
*news agent* that had some kinky advice.

## Nunny

Vagina
*Pronounced* *'noon·nee'*
<u>As in</u>: Girls, a dirty *nunny* is not a sexy
thing.

## Nutters

Crazy, mad person
*Pronounced* *'nut·erz*
<u>As in</u>: I must be *nutters* today because I
bought the ugliest dress at full price!

## Off license

Convenience store specializing in alcohol
sales
*Pronounced* *'off lie·cense'*
<u>As in</u>: Pick up some wine and dessert for me
at the *off license*.

# Oi

Hey
*Pronounced* *'oh ee'*
<u>As in</u>: *Oi*, catch the ball and don't let it smack you in the face.

## Old Bailey

A famous jail in London or just any jail
*Pronounced* *'old bay·lee'*
<u>As in</u>: Getting dragged to the *Old Bailey* in handcuffs is not my idea of fun any day.

## Old Bill

Police
*Pronounced* *'old bill'*
<u>As in</u>: The *old bill* arrested the bloke that stole my bag.

## On the missing

Laying low, being on your own and not wanting outside contact
*Pronounced* *'on the miss·in'*

As in: I will be *on the missing* for the next few weeks until exams are over so you may not hear from me.

## On the obo

Under surveillance, being watched by the police
*Pronounced* 'on the ob·bo'
As in: Since the robbery, then the neighborhood has been *on the obo*.

## Paddy

Irish person (may or may not be insulting)
*Pronounced* 'pah·dee'
As in: *Paddy* meat pies are the best despite what the Brits think.

## Party

Party
*Pronounced* 'pawtee'
As in: I had a wicked *party* for my hen night.

# Peeps

People
*Pronounced* 'peeps'
<u>As in</u>: The *peeps* and I are going to the City
for a Stag party.

# Pence

Penny
*Pronounced* 'pence'
<u>As in</u>: I'm so broke; I can't even find *pence*
under the cushions to buy some crisps.

# Pensioner

Old person who is about retirement age
*Pronounced* 'pen·shon·er'
<u>As in</u>: I think *pensioners* in Britain get free
bus and train passes after as part of their
senior benefits.

# Petrol

Gas
*Pronounced* 'peh·trol'
<u>As in</u>: I ran out of *petrol* and the car almost
didn't make it to mum's flat.

## Pictures

Movies
*Pronounced* 'pic·tures'
<u>As in</u>: Let's go to the *pictures* to see that new Batman film.

## Pig

Police
*Pronounced* 'pig'
<u>As in</u>: I can't believe the *pig* arrested me for knicking a few ice lollies.

## Pike

Londoner (often insulting), Gypsy (could be insulting)
*Pronounced* 'pie·kee'
<u>As in</u>: *Pikes* are the best people to show you around London.

## Pinch

Steal
*Pronounced* 'pin·che'
<u>As in</u>: Don't even try to *pinch* from the corner store, they have cameras.

# Pissed

Drunk
*Pronounced* 'pissed'
<u>As in</u>: I got so *pissed* at the pub last night I could hardly find my way home.

# Pop in

Stop by, go into
*Pronounced* 'pop in'
<u>As in</u>: There is a *half license* on the corner; please pop in and get a bottle of wine.

# Posh

Diva
*Pronounced* 'posh'
<u>As in</u>: Are you too *posh* to sit on the floor to watch telly even at home?

# Post

To mail something or the actual mail
*Pronounced* 'poost'
<u>As in</u>: Please *post* this letter for me on your way to work.
<u>As in</u>: Did you pick up the *post* when you came through the door?

## Pram

Baby stroller
*Pronounced* 'pram'
<u>As in</u>: Get the *pram* so I can strap the baby in to go shopping.

## Prat

Prick, jerk (could be joke or insult)
*Pronounced* 'prat'
<u>As in</u>: That *prat* took all my reddies from purse.

## Pub

Bar (the central hangout spot for most locals)
*Pronounced* 'pub'
<u>As in</u>: Ladies get free drinks at the *pub* on Wednesdays.

## Pucker

Good, really good
*Pronounced* 'puck·ah'
<u>As in</u>: That's *pucker,* I got the last tickets to the Man U match.

## Puffta

Gay guy (insulting)
*Pronounced* 'poof·tah'
As in: I can't say *pufftas* are my favorites but hey they can be colorful.

## Queue

Line of people (typically)
*Pronounced* 'que'
As in: The supermarket *queues* are ridiculously long on Sundays before a match.

## Quid

British money
*Pronounced* 'qwid'
As in: Give me five *quid* and I'll get you lunch.

## Randy

Horny, sexually aroused
*Pronounced* 'ran·dee'
As in: Do I make you *randy* baby?

# Rave

Party – often in an illegal location
*Pronounced* 'rayv'
<u>As in</u>:  The *rave* got broken up by the pigs
before it even got started.

# Reddies

Money
*Pronounced* 'red·eez'
<u>As in</u>:  My *reddies* are low this month
because I haven't been paid yet.

# Reg

Registration – as in your car license plate
*Pronounced* 'rej'
<u>As in</u>:  My I have to renew my *reg* before it
expires and I get a ticket.

# Rubbish

Garbage
*Pronounced* 'rub·eesh'
<u>As in</u>:  Take out the *rubbish* before it starts
to stink up the place.

# Rubbish

Nonsense, foolishness, gibberish
*Pronounced* 'rub·eesh'
As in: Stop talking *rubbish*; I don't believe a word you say.

# Sacked

Fired, let go from job
*Pronounced* 'sakt'
As in: I got *sacked* for getting my knickers in a bunch at the meeting.

# Sat nav

GPS
*Pronounced* 'sat nav'
As in: Without my *sat nav*, I'd never be able to find my way around without getting lost.

# Scabba

Slut – (could be a joke or insult)
*Pronounced* 'skab·ah'
As in: That dirty old *scabba* tried to hit on my man as if he'd want her nasty ass.

## Scoff

To eat a lot of food really fast
*Pronounced* 'skof'
<u>As in</u>: You *scoff* your food as if you haven't
eaten in years.

## Score

20 pound note
*Pronounced* 'skoore'
<u>As in</u>: I only need a *score* to get that new
top but mum won't buy it for me.

## Shag

Sex
*Pronounced* 'shag'
<u>As in</u>: I want to *shag* the first hot guy I
meet.

## Shattered

Tired
*Pronounced* 'shat·herd'
<u>As in</u>: I am *shattered* after taking both of
the kids to the park today.

## Shift-on

Hurry
*Pronounced* '*shift on*'
<u>As in</u>: Get a *shift on* with those dishes so
we can be ready for dinner.

## Shit stabber

Gay guy or general insult (insulting)
*Pronounced* '*shit stab·her*'
<u>As in</u>: That freaking *shit stabber* tried to
hit on my boyfriend in front of me!

## Sixth form

Year 12, since high school ends at year 11
*Pronounced* '*sixth form*'
<u>As in</u>: Getting into *sixth form* could help
prepare me for college if I can get in.

## Skatty

All over the place, unorganized
*Pronounced* '*skatty*'
<u>As in</u>: I've been so *skatty* lately; I can't find
anything in my room.

## Skaggy

Shabby, dirty
*Pronounced* 'skag·ee'
<u>As in</u>: Your *skaggy* jumper should be tossed out with the rubbish.

## Skint

Broke, lacking money
*Pronounced* 'skin·t'
<u>As in</u>: I'm totally *skint*, not even enough for a coffee.

## Slag

A woman who has a reputation for sleeping around
*Pronounced* 'slag'
<u>As in</u>: I can't believe the *slag* had the nerve to tell me that my skirt is short.

## Slapper

Slut (often insulting)
*Pronounced* 'slappa'

As in: That old *slapper* should have at least charged for sex, she could have made a lot of spondulis.

## Slash

Poop
*Pronounced* *'slash'*
As in: I need to take a *slash* so bad; that guacamole must have been bad.

## Sling

Throw
*Pronounced* *'sling'*
As in: *Sling* that shirt over here for me; I want to try it on.

## Smart

Dressed well
*Pronounced* *'smaat'*
As in: You look so *smart* in your new school uniform.

## Snog

Kiss
*Pronounced* 'zn·ogg'
<u>As in</u>: I can't believe that manky bloke tried to *snog* me; it was so gross.

## Solicitor

An attorney who doesn't go to court but instead hands a case requiring court appearance over to barrister
*Pronounced* 'so·lee·cit·or'
<u>As in</u>: I went to the *solicitor* for advice on how to evict my tenant.

## Sorted

Figured out
*Pronounced* 'sort·ed'
<u>As in</u>: I have the answers to the quiz are all *sorted*, so stop worrying.

## Spade

Black person (may be insulting)
*Pronounced* 'spayed'

As in: I don't think all Jamaican's are *spades*
despite what you've heard.

## Spin on a six pence

Bad temper
*Pronounced* 'spin on a six pence'
As in: Your *spin on a six pence* will only get
you an ass whupping.

## Spondulis

Money
*Pronounced* 'spon·doo·lis'
As in: With or without *spondulis*, I'm going
down to the pub tonight to grab a pint.

## Spud

Potato
*Pronounced* 'sp·hud'
As in: Grab me some *spuds* from the fridge
and I'll make fish and chips.

## Stag night or Stag party

Bachelor party
*Pronounced* 'stag night' or stag party'

As in: The boys had a wild stag night in Las Vegas and almost didn't make it back in time for the wedding.

## Stitches

Tickled with laughter
*Pronounced* 'stee·cheez'
As in: That joke was so funny it had me in stitches.

## Sum fink

Something
*Pronounced* 'some fink'
As in: I found *sum fink* wrong with my salad; there's a bug in it.

## Take the piss

To make fun of
*Pronounced* 'take the piss'
As in: Don't *take the piss* with me, you will regret it.

# Tart

Slut
*Pronounced* *'tar·tee'*
<u>As in</u>: That *tart* refused to stop flirting with my old man even though I was right there.

# Tea

Dinner
*Pronounced* *'tee'*
<u>As in</u>: For *tea*, I will bring some wine and a casserole.

# Telly

TV
*Pronounced* *'tell·ee'*
<u>As in</u>: I want to catch Britain's Got Talent on *telly* tonight.

# Tenner

10 pound note
*Pronounced* *'tenn·a'*
<u>As in</u>: I need a *tenner* top up my mobile.

## The mickey

Make fun of
_Pronounced_ 'the mik·ee'
<u>As in</u>:  I don't like when you make _the mickey_ of me.

## The old man

Boyfriend
_Pronounced_ 'the old man'
<u>As in</u>:  _The old man_ tried to get me to stay home with him instead of going raving.

## Till

Cash register (cashier)
_Pronounced_ 'til'
<u>As in</u>:  The bloke at the shop _till_ keeps smiling at me.

## To let

For rent (property)
_Pronounced_ 'to let'
<u>As in</u>:  There are no decent flats _to let_ in this area.

# Toilet

Restroom
*Pronounced* *'toy·let'*
<u>As in</u>:  The *toilets* at the club are always the nastiest.

# Top

Shirt
*Pronounced* *'top'*
<u>As in</u>:  Let's pop into the shops and pick up a *top* for the rave tonight.

# Top up

To add credit to your pay-as-you-go phone
*Pronounced* *'top up'*
<u>As in</u>:  Spare me a cockle to *top up* mi phone.

# Tosser

A person who masturbates; a rude person; a stupid person
*Pronounced* *'toss·a'*
<u>As in</u>:  Rich's such a *tosser*, he doesn't know his ass from his ears.

## Trainer

Sneakers
*Pronounced* 'train·a'
<u>As in</u>: J.D. Sport has Nike *trainers* on sale.

## Travel cot

Baby bassinet; baby car seat
*Pronounced* 'travel cot'
<u>As in</u>: Grab the baby's *travel cot* and put it in the boot.

## Trousers

Pants
*Pronounced* 'trow·zas'
<u>As in</u>: Mi *trousers* got muddy at gran's allotment.

## Tube

Subway train
*Pronounced* 'chube'
<u>As in</u>: You know if the *tube* schedule is gonna change because of the bank holiday?

## TV license

An annual fee for having and using television service.  The government has monitoring vehicles that go around to ensure that those watching telly paid their fees.
*Pronounced* *'tee·vee lie·sense'*
As in:  I better pay my *TV license* so I can watch my shows without thinking I'm going to be fined.

## Underground

Subway station
*Pronounced* *'under·ground'*
As in:  Hey let's take the *underground* to the rave in East End.

## Uni

University
*Pronounced* *'you·nee'*
As in:  Getting into a good *uni* can be like winning the lotto.

## Up the duff

Pregnant
*Pronounced* 'up the duff'
As in: Are you getting fat or are you *up the duff*?

## Wanger

Money
*Pronounced* 'wang·ah'
As in: Mi *wangers* are fresh out how am I to get to the knees up tonight?

## Wank

To masturbate; a jerk
*Pronounced* 'wank'
As in: Why *wank* when you there're so many slags to bunkup with?

## Wanker

A person who masturbates; a rude person; a stupid person
*Pronounced* 'wang·ka'
As in: You're such a *wanker* for slapping around that bloke in front of his bird.

## Wasp in a jam jar

Angry and can't do anything about it
*Pronounced* 'wasp in a jam jar'
<u>As in</u>: Stop being such a *wasp in a jam jar.*
Anger is pointless unless you're gonna
apologize.

## Well fit

Pretty, sexy, hot, (male or female)
*Pronounced* 'well fit'
<u>As in</u>: That sista is *well fit,* I fancy a
bunkup with her.

## Whizz

To blend; to make something quickly
*Pronounced* 'wiz'
<u>As in</u>: I have to *whizz* up some food for the
party tonight.

## Wicked

Amazing, awesome
*Pronounced* 'wik·id'
<u>As in</u>: That was a *wicked* party last night. I
didn't get home until noon.

## Willy

Penis
*Pronounced* 'will·ee'
<u>As in</u>: Some men will stick their *willy* into any hole they find.

## Wind up

Act of intentionally working to get someone angry or someone who typically likes to piss others off
*Pronounced* 'wined up'
<u>As in</u>: You are such a *wind up*. Don't think you can *wind up* someone and avoid getting an ass kicking.

## Wobbly bits

Fatty body parts that jiggle
*Pronounced* 'wob·lee bitz'
<u>As in</u>: My *wobbly bits* are off limits unless you're mi old man.

## Yank

American person
*Pronounced* 'yank'

As in: *Yanks* love to party this side of the Pond.

## Yardie

Jamaican person
*Pronounced* *'yawd·ee'*
As in: *Yardie* food is jerk chicken and rice, not bangers and mash.

## You lot

All of you
*Pronounced* *'you lot'*
As in: *You lot* better clean up this mess or I'm gonna clean the floor with you.

# Places and Parkology

### Chessington World of Adventures

Family oriented adventure park with lots of fun rides (roller coasters included) and a zoo located approximately 12 miles (19km) south of Central London. The park includes a safari themed resort hotel and family special prices.

http://www.chessington.com/

### Brighton

This gorgeous seaside town located in the Sussex countryside has been a haven for Brits from as far back as the 1800s. This was the destination where British aristocrats went to unwind. Today you will find kite surfing, amazing cathedrals, a beautiful beach, country houses, castles, parks, forts and gardens among a host of other attractions.

### Black Pool

Think offbeat Orbitecture (art revolution), theater, sightseeing, relaxation and the beach. Places to check out: Fleetwood Market, Pasaje Del Terror, Marine Hall, Central Pier, Grundy Art Gallery, Freeport

Fleetwood Outlet Village, Alien Attack, Sea Life Black Pool etc...

## Alton Towers

Britain's largest theme park and resort boasts a water park, spas, hotels and a host of other attractions.
http://www.altontowers.com/

## Margate

Being an island nation with sometimes dreary winters, Britain's seaside resorts hold a special allure especially at summertime. Margate is holds special memories for many Brits who recall childhoods spent surfing, jet skiing, kite-boarding or simply eating fish and chips by the shore. This is a timeless place that has been a haunt of Brits for centuries and is located in East Kent in the Thanet district about 38 miles (61 km) east-northeast of Maidstone.

Must see:
- Quex Museum, House and Gardens (in Birchington near Margate)
- Shell Grotto
- Strokes Adventure Golf
- Big Sky Jazz Festival (July)
- Thanet Coast Project
- Margate's Big Event (June)

## Madame Tussauds

Just a two minute walk from the Baker Street tube station on Marylebone Road in central London lies the premier wax museum in the world. Here you will find a replica of every noteworthy person in current entertainment and modern history. Prepare to be amazed.

## The Dungeons (aka London Dungeon)

There are actually five Dungeons: The London Dungeon, The Edinburgh Dungeon, The York Dungeon, The Amsterdam Dungeon and Hamburg Dungeon. The London Dungeon is the most renowned and is a freaking scary place because everything you see and learn relates to actual history not a Hollywood fantasy. Think tortures, gory and macabre historical events and you will be in your element.

## Thorpe Park

The second most visited amusement/theme park in the UK offers over 30 extreme rides and attractions. Among its major rides are the Nemesis Inferno (inverted roller coaster), Colossus, SAW: The Ride, Stealth, Tidal Wave and Vortex.
http://www.thorpepark.com/

## Legoland

A Lego themed theme park located in Windsor, England (about 8 miles west of Heathrow airport) with roller coasters and other attractions geared mainly toward young families with milder rides than other parks.  There are actually four similarly themed parks: Legoland Billund (Billund, Denmark), Legoland Windsor (Windsor, England), Legoland Deutschland (Gunzburg, Germany), and Legoland California (Carlsbad, San Diego California, USA).

## London Eye

The London Eye is a 443 ft (135 metre) high ferris wheel located on the bank of the Thames between Westminster Bridge and Hungerford Bridge.  This giant observation wheel provides an excellent way to see the City and offers an unparalleled view of the skyline day or night (providing the weather is clear).

## Warwick Castle

Built in 1068 by William the Conqueror it originally served as a fortification and was traditionally owned by the Earl of Warwick. This medieval castle in the county town of Warwickshire sits on the River Avon and has a storied history.

## Hyde Park

Hyde Park is a lush green 350 acre park located in the heart of London. This park is the destination for summer concerts, year round picnics and more activities than can be listed here. This is a beautiful locale that is open to visitors from 5am to midnight all year round – a definite must see.

## Greenwich Park

Think Greenich Mean Time and you this is the place where the Prime Meridian passes through. Located in Greenwich, this place evokes memories of summers spent playing football (UK football), flying kites, roller-blading, lying on the grass listening to concerts and daydreaming...

## Other Parks worth visiting:
http://www.royalparks.gov.uk/

Crystal Palace
Kensington Gardens
The Regents Park
Richmond Park
St. James Park
Busy Park
Green Park
Brompton Cemetery

# Bargain Shopology

**Fleetwood Market**

Bustling traditional marketplace located in Fleetwood that offers a local shopping experience with over 200 indoor stalls in three heated halls and 50 outdoor stalls

**Petticoat Lane**

Located near to Liverpool Street tube station off Middlesex Street, Petticoat Lane is a fantastic place to shop and find great bargains.

**Finsbury Park**

Located in Islington, this market is open daily but Saturday is the main shopping day.

**Camden Market**

Located in Camden Town, London, this market offers over a 1,000 open-air shops, pubs and restaurants (above and below ground level).  This market is open 364 days except for Christmas and can be reached by bus, above ground (train), train etc...

## Oxford Street

There are over 548 phenomenal shops located near the Oxford Street tube station. This West End shopping mecca is nothing short of spectacular and a must see even if you are merely browsing.

## Knightsbridge

If bargain shopping is not really your thing then is the place to be. This is a higher-end shopper's paradise. This exclusive ritzy area is home to some of the wealthiest Londoners and boast equally impressive shopping options among which are the famed Harrods and Harvey Nichols.

## East Street Market (aka The Lane)

East Street Market is a bargain shoppers dream! Located in Walworth, South London between Old Kent Road and Walworth Road, the Lane is an open-air shopping haunt of locals from far and near. As with all the other markets highlighted, you can find everything from fresh fruits and vegetables to name brand clothing, luggage and sometimes small furniture.

**Brixton Market**

Brixton Market, located in Brixton, South London, is an excellent place to find fresh fruits and vegetables, meats, clothes and an assortment of odds and ends. This market is a mixture of open-air stalls and covered shopping areas.

**Peckham Market**

Another farmer's market off Peckham High Street is a great place to stock up on your fresh produce. Feel free to browse the local shops along the street as well like a true Londoner.

www.ingramcontent.com/pod-product-compliance
Lightning Source LLC
Chambersburg PA
CBHW021244280526
45784CB00005B/2231